1602™

WRITER: **NEIL GAIMAN**
ILLUSTRATOR: **ANDY KUBERT**
DIGITAL PAINTING: **RICHARD ISANOVE**
LETTERING: **TODD KLEIN**
COVER ARTIST: **SCOTT McKOWEN**

ASSISTANT EDITOR: **NICK LOWE**
MANAGING EDITOR: **NANCI DAKESIAN**
ASSITANT MANAGING EDITOR: **KELLY LAMY**
EDITOR IN CHIEF: **JOE QUESADA**
PRESIDENT: **DAN BUCKLEY**

MARVEL® GRAPHIC NOVEL presents **1602**

MARVEL 1602. Contains material originally published in magazine form as 1602 Vol. 1 #1-8. Second impression; first impression 2002. Published by Panini Publishing, a division of Panini UK Limited. Mike Riddell, Managing Director. Alan O'Keefe, Managing Editor. Mark Irvine, Production Manager. Marco M. Lupoi, Publishing Director Europe. Brady Webb, Reprint Editor. Caroline Dunk, Designer. Office of publication: Panini House, Coach & Horses Passage, The Pantiles, Tunbridge Wells, Kent TN2 5UJ. Tel: 01892 500 100. First printing 2004 Copyright © 2003, 2004 by Marvel Characters, Inc. All rights reserved. No similarity between any of the names, characters, persons and/or institutions in this magazine with any living or dead person or institution is intended, and any similarity which may exist is purely coincidental. This publication may not be sold except by authorised dealers and is sold subject to the conditions that it shall not be sold or distributed with any part of its cover or markings removed, nor in a mutilated condition. MARVEL 1602 (including all prominent characters featured in this issue and the distinctive likeness thereof) is a trademark of MARVEL CHARACTERS, INC. and this publication is under license from Marvel Characters, Inc. through Panini S.p.A. Printed in Italy. ISBN:1-904159-43-5

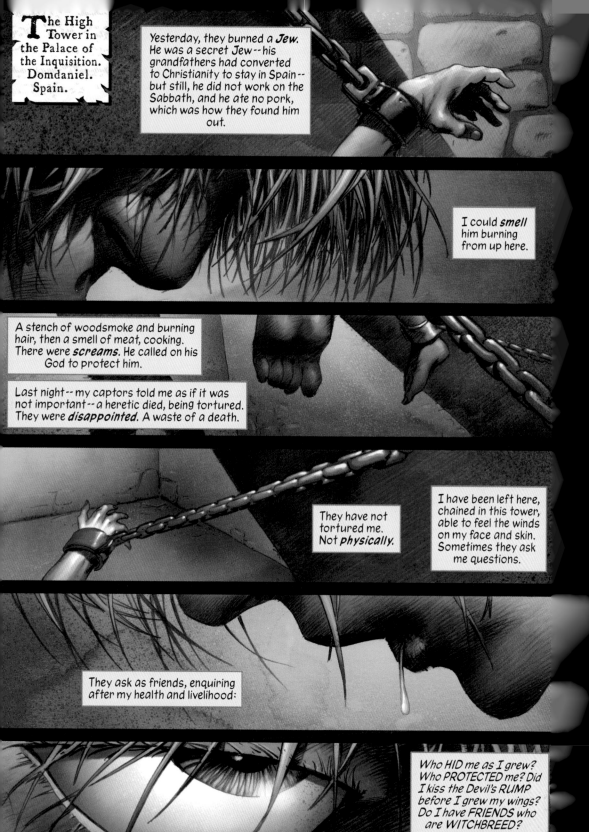

The High Tower in the Palace of the Inquisition. Domdaniel. Spain.

Yesterday, they burned a *Jew*. He was a secret Jew -- his grandfathers had converted to Christianity to stay in Spain -- but still, he did not work on the Sabbath, and he ate no pork, which was how they found him out.

I could *smell* him burning from up here.

A stench of woodsmoke and burning hair, then a smell of meat, cooking. There were *screams*. He called on his God to protect him.

Last night -- my captors told me as if it was not important -- a heretic died, being tortured. They were *disappointed*. A waste of a death.

They have not tortured me. Not *physically*.

I have been left here, chained in this tower, able to feel the winds on my face and skin. Sometimes they ask me questions.

They ask as friends, enquiring after my health and livelihood:

Who HID me as I grew? Who PROTECTED me? Did I kiss the Devil's RUMP before I grew my wings? Do I have FRIENDS who are WITCHBREED?

I have lived for almost seventeen years. I *die* tomorrow. And this is what hurts the most: that I shall die on the *ground*. That I shall never take to the skies again, to dance, to laugh, to *fly*...

Or rather, that when I take to the skies, for one last time, it will be as *ashes*.

I see a **tower**. And in the tower there is...an **angel**.

No. No, I lie. It is a **man**. A **man** with wings.

They are piling **firewood** in the square below. The square is filled with ghosts in pain, who scream in silent voices, trapped in their final moments...

Who **does** this thing, Stephen? What is its **significance?**

Would that I knew...

Nothing, Grand Inquisitor. Perhaps...perhaps I simply *imagined* it.

I *doubt* it.

No, it was *Javier.* I have no doubt on *that* score.

Petros? Send a message to the guard: they must be *extra* vigilant at tomorrow's burning.

Yes sir.

You may *leave* us, Sister Wanda.

So *tell* me, Petros, *how* was the court of James of Scotland?

His Majesty sends you his *greetings,* Inquisitor.

And?

While James is of the *Protestant* faith, he feels that there is common cause against...

"...witches, magicians and the witchbreed, who infest England like lice crawling through a shepherd's crotch."

His words. Not mine.

So is there room for an *alliance?*

He told me that the English have *long* memories. They have not yet forgotten Queen Mary -- they call her Bloody Mary -- and her burnings.

He says that *any* work must be done *carefully* and *quietly* -- and with public support and approval.

Why have we come *this* way, Sir Nicholas? Why are we *here*?

Ah. A very *profound* question, Peter. Why *are* we here? To *suffer*, some say. Others claim that this world is a refining fire in which the dross in our souls--

No, I mean, um, *here*, by the *Temple*. Should we not be crossing the *river*?

Not at *all*. This is a perfect place to be. We are here for two reasons.

Firstly because it was built by the *Templars*, four hundred years ago. And what do we know of the Templars, *eh*, Peter?

I don't know much about *monks* and such, Sir Nicholas. Before my *time*.

If you are to prosper, in this world of secrets and powers, you must understand *many* things that happened before your time.

How else can we understand our *own* time, or predict what may come?

I...

I see. Yes. Your point is taken, sir.

Please-- *who* were the Templars?

That is a small *question*, but with as many *answers* as a hydra has heads.

In brief, they were an order of *warrior monks,* founded, some five hundred years ago, to *guard* the routes to Jerusalem.

Queen Elizabeth is an old woman, and in pain, and she sleeps poorly. Now she tosses uncomfortably in her bed, and rolls over, and dreams a strange dream.

The Old Man left Jerusalem two days ago, in a cart, pulled by a donkey. The back of the cart was piled high with battered furniture — chairs, and pots, and an unremarkable wooden chest — and padded with straw.

As he left, three other carts left Jerusalem. The other carts were accompanied by outriders, and guards. They were decoys, although the men who drove them did not know that.

The Old Man is accompanied only by a member of their order who can pass as a deaf-mute servant.

The rumble of the storm is now almost continual.

He knows much, the Old Man. He knows many things.

He knows that one of the other three carts has already been seized by enemies, by those who would steal the treasures of their order.

He felt them die.

How are you *feeling*?

Terrified. And, um, *sea-sick*.

But happy not to have been burned to death.

Who *are* you people? How did you get into the *fortress*? How do you do that thing with your *eyes*? And that wall of *ice*? And why does the boat go so *fast* without a sail?

And where are we *going*?

You are *all* questions, my friend.

And I would like some *answers*.

Very well. Who *are* we? We are *witchbreed*, like you.

I am Apprentice *Scotius Summerisle*, this is journeyman *Robert Trefusis,* and over there, at the helm of this craft, is Apprentice *John Grey.*

He speaks but little.

It is *he* that propels us through these seas, without wind or current.

We are almost in English waters. It is time to remove our robes. Monks are not welcome in England. *Fishermen,* on the other hand, will attract no attention.

Your *chest...?*

They *brand* monsters, where I come from, before they *drown* them.

Can you hide your *wings?*

I can *fold* them, to hide beneath my garb. And my mother made me clothes with room for them--she sewed them so cunningly that no man could tell.

They *killed* her, you know, when they *caught* me.

They said, *come back, or we kill her,* so I came back. But they killed her anyway.

I'm sorry.

We have garb for you, and cords to bind your wings.

Our master thinks of everything. We shall dock by noon, and a horse-cart will be waiting to take us the rest of the way.

As to where we *go,* we are on our way to a *schoolhouse,* which we call *Sanctuary.* And it is there that our master and our teacher will answer the *rest* of your questions.

And it is there that we shall be *safe* from the *world?*

Aye. *Perhaps.*

For *a little* while.

From Sir Nicholas Fury to Her Majesty Elizabeth, By the Grace of God, Greetings.

Madam,

Since last we spoke, I have despatched my finest agent to the continent. He journeys to meet the Old Man, the Head of the Templars, who has smuggled the treasure of the Templars out of Jerusalem. My man, whom I have only encountered in darkness, will bring him and his treasure to our shores safely.

The Strange weather continues, putting many in fear of their lives.

Today, Miss Virginia Dare, the first born of Your Majesty's Colony in Roanoke, will be presented to Your Majesty. I have entrusted my attendant, Master Parquagh, with her safety.

I will not be there, alas. It has become imperative that I speak to the learned Carlos Javier, whose educational establishment I have discussed with you on many prior occasions.

I shall take pleasure in ensuring Your Majesty at all times knows what transpires.

And have the honour to sign myself,

Sir Nicholas Fury

Thus I was left alone in the world, possessed of nothing but my *wits,* which are sharper than those who see my face would credit...

...and men would call me *beast* or *troll* and fling muck and stones at me, until I found that, in strength and agility, I was master of them all.

A creature of few words, then?

Sir Nicholas *jests.* And yet, in your jest is *truth,* for I am famed for speaking only when words are called for, and otherwise I am silent as the grave.

Do not talk of *graves,* my fine beast. Not today.

No, sire. Please wait here.

Nicholas! What *are* you doing?

A noxious weed, Nicholas. *Please,* put it out, it fouls the air and blackens the lungs.

The last man to tell me that was King James of Scotland. Who'd have thought that you and he would ever *agree,* Carlos?

And why would *James* concern himself with a little school for the sons of Gentlefolk?

If you think he'll not find you all, Carlos, you're *dreaming.*

The Inquisition are on your trail. They may hate James, but they hate you more.

Talking about the Inquisition, I understand that you stole a new pupil from under their noses last week.

Our *Angel?* How did you...?

Your pardon-- I forget. You are *Her Majesty's Intelligence.* If it concerns the safety of the kingdom, a *butterfly* will not fall that you do not hear about.

So why are you here?

To beg a favour. And to *warn* you. Time is not kind to the Queen. James will soon be King of England, as well as Scotland.

And if there's one thing James *hates* more than he hates tobacco, it's *witches.*

So our time of safety will end. *Omnia mutantur.* Everything changes.

The common people call us witchbreed, but there is no *magic* to what we do, Nicholas.

Pick me up. Carry me out to the gardens.

London. The Bleeding Heart Inn.

I am here to see Mistress *Dare.* Is she within?

Rojhaz? I thought I *heard* somebody--

Sir? Oh, *sir!*

Madam... your savage... my hand...

I am...here from...the Queen...

Rojhaz! Let him *go!*

I beg your forgiveness, sir-- he thinks only to *protect* me.

ROJHAZ!

I must *apologize*, sir. Rojhaz is my bodyguard--he has been so since I was a babe; indeed my father says that without him our colony would never have survived its first winter...

I am *babbling!* You are from the *Queen?*

Yes, lady. This afternoon the Queen will receive you at Hampton Court. I was sent to bring you safely to her--

Rojhaz come also.

I am afraid that I was not instructed to bring anyone else, only Miss Dare--

Rojhaz come.

Er... no...

Put him *down.* You will wait here for me, Rojhaz. Do you *hear* me?

You see... I was told to bring Mistress Virginia... Sir Nicholas said nothing about anyone else...

...but... I'm certain...that he would hate to see... Mistress Virginia parted from her bodyguard...

Rojhaz come.

Good.

Not of darkness, and then, when he saw the green glow, not of that.

It oozed down the walls, and it seemed to pulse as he looked at it. It burned like green fire. He had never seen anything like it.

Beyond that, the caverns were in darkness. He kept walking.

And when he felt the fresh sea air on his face, and felt the pebbles crunch beneath his feet, and heard the sea and the cries of the gulls, he knew he was outside.

His mother had found him there on the beach, fevered and muttering about the darkness and the night.

He thought it somehow the dead of night, as he fell to the beach, and slept.

It was a night that was never

The Court of King James the Sixth of Scotland.

I had a *dream*, you know, David...

I dreamed that these dark rains and floods and earthquakes, they are the *anger* of *God*, because we suffer *witches* to live among us. The anger of God is a *terrible* thing.

A fearsome dream indeed, Majesty.

The Inquisitor's man wishes to speak to you.

The *pretty* man? Back so soon? Very well, David. Show him in.

Greetings, Your Majesty. I relayed your wishes to the Grand Inquisitor, and I have an answer for you.

You *do*? That was damned fast. How'd you get a message to Spain and back in what, a couple of days?

I ran very fast, Sire.

Haha! I *like* you, sir. A *fine* jest. "*Ran very fast.*"

Well, and what does the Inquisitor say?

He **accepts** your terms. He says to tell you that once you are King, he will have the English crying out for the **blood** of the **witchbreed**. He says to tell you that they will be **begging** you to light the bonfires.

And he said one **more** thing -- that when that day comes, Javier and all his demonic brood of **witches** and **monsters** must be delivered to the Inquisitor **personally** to be dealt with. They are not to be hurt, except by **us**.

I see...

But if my dream is true, then she would need to die **very** soon. If Providence destroyed the Isles of Britain before I could be King, that would be a terribly **bad** thing.

Will you tell your Master **that**?

Are you asking me to tell him that the Queen of England has lived too long?

That would be a **dreadful** thing to say, laddie.

But **aye**... she's an old woman. And the sooner she was to die, the more friendly I would be to your master.

I see. Very well. I shall **tell** him.

Will you not stay and drink a dram of **wine** with me, pretty man?

Alas, I **cannot**. I must run fast, to give the Inquisitor your message.

A **funny man!** Hurry back to me with his reply.

My father was *sad* when he sent me here. He called me *the Luck of the Colony.*

But if there is truly a Luck of the Colony, it is Rojhaz. *He* found us that first winter, when we were *starving,* and he hunted game for us, and *fed* us. We would have *died...*

What did your *mother* think of you coming all this way?

My mother is *dead,* Master Peter. She took an ague and passed away when I was an infant.

And *you?* How did you come into the Queen's service?

My mother and father... *also* passed away. I lived with my Aunt and Uncle.

On my last birthday Sir Nicholas Fury came to the door. He had known my parents. He said it was time that I entered his service, and that it was what my father would have wished.

My Uncle Benjamin was *delighted* for me. My aunt wept and bade me to write to her, and return when I could.

And what do you *do* for Sir Nicholas?

I do what he *tells* me.

And is that what you *want* to do?

I would love to *make* things.

I once watched a drop of dew in a spider's web, magnifying the blade of grass behind it. Which made me *think*, some of us can see like hawks, but many of us can *not*, and if I were to grind some glass to the shape of the dewdrop...

I am sorry. I must be *boring* you.

I am in my appointed place. I send money back to my uncle and my aunt. I do my *duty*.

You should come to the New World, Master Peter. In our colony, we *need* people who can make things.

Greenwich. The House of Doctor Stephen Strange.

Hmm. I shall need a fishing *net*. And a *black* candle, and a *red* candle.

And *chalk*.

Stephen? What are you *doing?*

Going to the palace.

Why?

I have *absolutely* no idea.

Your pupils are *remarkable*, Carlos.

Yes. They are.

Why did you *show* me this? If I were to report to Her Majesty that the refugees and orphans we quietly welcomed in to our shores are a team of *soldiers* beyond our imaginings...

It would mean my *head?* Perhaps. But the Queen knows I am *loyal* to her.

If she believes that, Carlos, she is *wrong*. And if *you* believe that, you are fooling yourself.

What do *you* think, Master Grey?

He is right, Master.

Your loyalty is to the *Witchbreed*, not to England. Just as *ours* is to you.

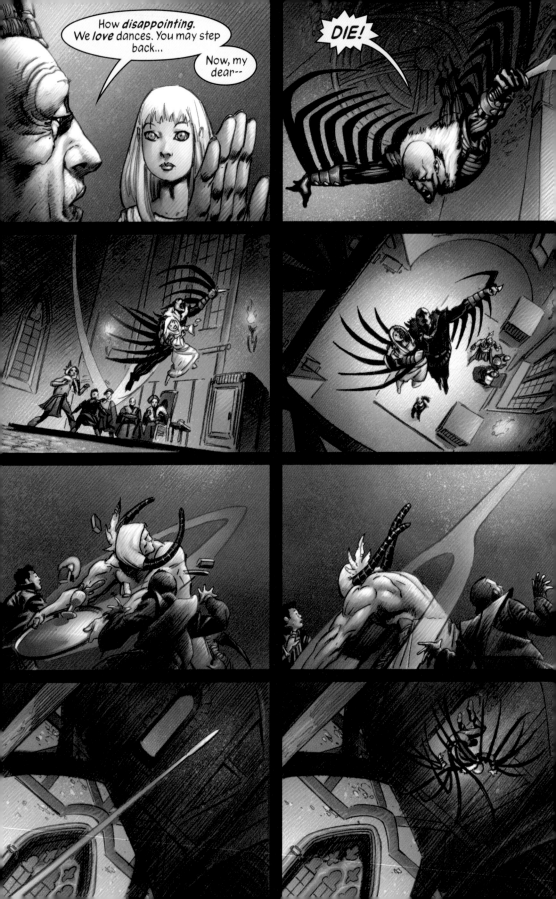

Virginia! Where did she go?

And what happened to his face?

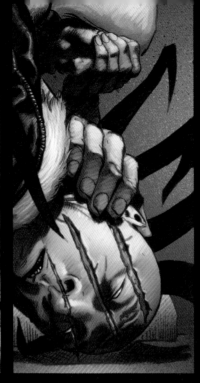

"Where's Virginia?!"

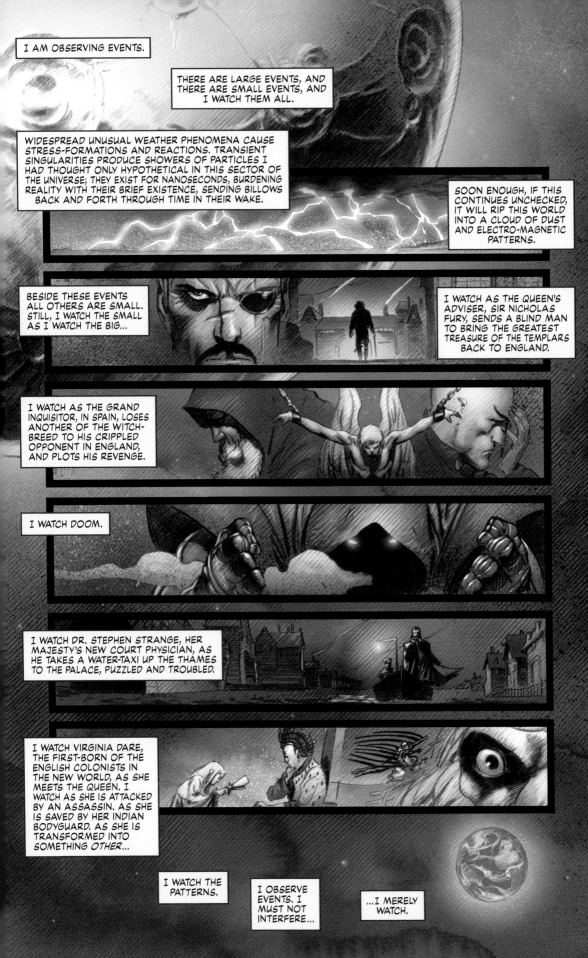

Where *is* she?

Up.

Up on the *roof?* There must be a way up there.

Yes... we climb. Come.

I can't climb.

You must be her bodyguard. I am a *friend.* Do you believe me?

I... Rojhaz. Yes. Friend.

Then you must answer me honestly.

Is she likely to be *dangerous?*

...yes.

I see. Well, we must do what we can.

There are **no** fresh horses waiting here Fraulein. No driver. **Nothing.** I **told** you.

But our horses are exhausted. They can't keep going...

I am **sorry**, Mein Herr. There have been such rains in the last few days, your horses are not here. The roads run like rivers.

But think, if the horses cannot get here, then your carriage **also** cannot get through. I am sure that as soon as the ways to the south are passable once more you will be on your way.

Meanwhile, you must **stay here.**

We have no rooms free-- there are soldiers here, waiting for the rains to stop. But you can sleep above the stables...

No. We have no time.

Well, you'll not be going anywhere until these storms are over.

Of course it's the wrath of God! **When** have we had such weather as this?

Aye-- they say there was a **firestorm** in Prague...

Matthew-- the soldiers he spoke of. They're over there.

I can **hear** them, Natasha. I am **blind,** not deaf.

Captain...a **business** proposition. I would very much like to **buy** your best horses.

She is **beautiful.** I'll say **that** for her.

I repeat. I will **pay** for the horses.

You. Blind man. What do you do?

Me? I sing for your lordship's pleasure, General.

Show us.

So they looks at themselves as they steps onto land, And they knew that their lives had been saved.

Then each of the four of them puts out a hand...

And they touched, and gave thanks, standing there on the sand, For the fortune that favours the brave, the brave--

For fortune still favours the--

Enough! And this madwoman. Is she your mistress? Or does she also sing?

Not at all. She can't sing a note.

She's the most dangerous woman in Europe.

Honestly, Colonel, you'd better sell her your horses.

Blind man! You are very funny...

Peter. You are to go immediately to Strange, and take him to Mistress Dare's rooms. He is to attend her. Queen's orders.

Good evening, Ambassador.

What's that?

A *gift* for Her Majesty. It plays sweet music, without human hand.

Remarkable. What will Count Otto come up with *next?* Eh, Peter?

I trust the Queen will *enjoy* it.

When you get to the girl's rooms, you are *not* to leave them alone together, do you understand me? Listen to *everything*. Tell me *everything*.

Of course, Sir Nicholas.

"If you need me tonight, I shall be in the Tower. I need answers."

My *lady*. Are you the *Doctor's wife?*

I have that honour, lad. And you are?

Peter. Peter Parquagh, mistress. I am here to fetch the Doctor. It's on the Queen's business.

He is in his study. Wait *here*, Peter.

A strange place, my lady...

These are creatures from all across the face of the world, brought here for the Doctor, for his potions and his love of knowledge.

Eye of newt and toe of bat, all that?

Not in the way you imagine it. That fish, for example, when dried and ground, causes a man to become insensible and to feel no pain.

A great boon to *any* physician.

Wait *here*. I shall get the Doctor.

Do not move, Peter.

I--I'm not scared. He's very lovely.

I believe he's actually a *she*. And yes. She *is*.

She was a gift from poor Sir Reed, God rest his soul... he sent her back from his travels, what, five years ago now?

Before your time.

Sometimes, like him, she still goes exploring.

She's *venomous*. But in her venom there are many secrets. And she'll not bite *me*, would you, dear?

"So, Peter, I take it the Queen wishes me to attend Miss Dare?"

"How did you *know?* I said nothing about that."

"I am a magician, boy, have you forgotten? And Sir Nicholas is quite predictable."

You will not talk. Your friend is in no state to talk. I want information.

So I'm not going to torture you.

I'm going to offer you a deal.

Last week you tried to kill me. You failed. Your knife broke on my chainmail. I'm sure that was a bitter disappointment.

I'm offering you a second chance. You'll have a blade. I will be unarmed. If you kill me...

...you can take the key to this cell from my corpse, and vanish into the night.

And if I win, you talk.

Trick.

Ah, you *can* talk. No, no trick.

Do we have a deal?

...deal.

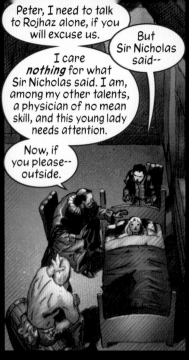

Peter, I need to talk to Rojhaz alone, if you will excuse us.

But Sir Nicholas said--

I care *nothing* for what Sir Nicholas said. I am, among my other talents, a physician of no mean skill, and this young lady needs attention.

Now, if you please-- outside.

She is in a ...ver. Her skin is ...urning up.

...numb ...whir am. ...numbu...

Has this happened before? A yes or no answer will suffice.

...yes.

Does anyone know about this? Apart from you.

...no.

She changes when scared?

...I... think... yes.

When did this start?

Five year... or six...

Does she always become that...winged creature?

White deer...white horse, also.

White

And is she usually this ill, afterward?

No. Was ill... not...not this bad...

Whatever's happening to the world. The weather... the madness.

It has its roots in this room, Rojhaz.

"What is she, Rojhaz? What *is* she?"

Who...

...sent...

...you?

TELL ME!

As for what happened to you, perhaps we should save that until my husband returns.

He has many questions for you.

Did I hurt anyone?

No, dear. Not really.

Oh.

We've all worried so. The Indian slept by your bed, and would barely leave your side.

And Fury's boy Peter was here, until yesterday.

She's awake, Stephen!

Hello Rojhaz.

Mistress Strange says that you made me soup. I'm very hungry.

Soup... hot. Burn hot.

I'll let it cool. I promise.

Ah, yes, *Fury.* Poor dead Gloriana's spymaster.

Well, have your spies told you who did this monstrous thing?

Agents of Count Otto von Doom, of Latveria, Majesty.

And have you any *evidence* for this...this dreadful accusation?

The word of another assassin.

I learned that a murder was planned, but not quickly enough to foil it.

I see. Well, *I* can educate you--

Master Banner? Where are you? Have you the paper? Well, give it here, man.

You see, Fury, what killed her most wondrous Majesty Elizabeth, by the grace of God Queen of England, was...

...the servants of the Devil.

There's a so-called school near Warwick.

I've the address here. It's a gathering place for all creatures of darkness in this land.

Merely by allowing it to exist, we are traitors to our country and our God.

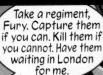

Take a regiment, Fury. Capture them if you can. Kill them if you cannot. Have them waiting in London for me.

Their leader is a monster called Javier. I am told that he can cloud minds, make people see things that are not there, even tell what men are thinking.

Go now. Take as many men as you'll need.

And Sir Nicholas...

Yes, Your Majesty?

Ye did a piss-poor job of protecting the Queen of England.

If you make a mess of *this,* you might as well walk to the Tower, and pick out a room wi' a view. D'you understand me?

Perfectly, Your Majesty.

"I was born just after they landed in the New World, fourteen years ago...

"My father says that it was a miracle that we survived, the first year. We did not know what to eat. We were colonists in a hostile wilderness. We did not know who our friends were, nor who our enemies.

There was no food. The crops they planted did not grow in me, and the animals were so hard to find...

"The year before we came, Sir Walter Raleigh had tried to set up a colony on Roanoke Island-- it had lasted only a few months, but those settlers had been cruel to the local Indians, and they have long memories...

"We almost starved. But then, one day, several Indians arrived, with Rojhaz at their head. They saw our plight, and returned several hours later with turkeys, and a deer, and grain.

"The people of the settlement ate that day and through that winter, with the help of their friends. In the spring the other Indians moved on, but Rojhaz stayed.

"My father says that he was the settlement's guardian angel. He told us when to plant, helped us build, taught our people to hunt. When we were attacked by leather-wings-- huge ones, bigger than eagles, much bigger than the kind you have here-- he helped to drive them off..."

"After the Spanish killed Sir Walter Raleigh and my grandfather, our first governor, on their way back to us from England, our little colony was almost forgotten.

"We had much to contend with-- the new land, and the strange weather, which scared almost all of the native people away from that area. But always, with the help of Rojhaz, we survived.

"And then...

"Rojhaz took a few of us across to the mainland, to trade some of our fish and crops for meat. I was eight, the other children were younger. And while my father and the rest of them smoked their pipes, I wandered off with my friends, across the marshes. I climbed some rocks.

"There was something hanging in the air. Something that glittered. You may think me foolish, but I could almost see it better with my eyes closed. It was so beautiful, like a gossamer veil, that glittered and gleamed and twisted.

"And I *touched* it...

"When I came to... Rojhaz had found me. He'd tracked me all across the marshes. He said that the others said there was a white flash, and that Jackie Harvie had said that where I was, a fawn had been. The others laughed at him.

"Rojhaz hunted the fawn, and waited until nightfall, when I became myself once more..."

"That was the first time I changed. It's happened twice since then-- each time when I was upset or angered. Once into some kind of lion. Once into a white horse.

"Each time Rojhaz found me, and brought me back safely."

And your father does not know?

Nobody knows. Only Rojhaz.

For most of my lifetime it felt as if our colony had been forgotten. The strange storms discouraged ships and new settlers as badly as the stories about the giant thunder-lizards of the plains.

We've scraped by as best we could, but we need more people. We need help.

That was why Ananias, my father, sent me to England. He wanted me to ask the Queen to invest money in the colony. He wanted me to try to raise support for more colonists to come to the Americas...

The strange weather only started here in the British Isles less than a year ago. Yet you say it has always been there where you are.

No. It started shortly before the first colonists landed. Then it spread across the Americas.

And now it covers the world. Virginia, I want you to come to my house in Greenwich. I can protect you there, more easily than I can protect you here...

But Stephen, Sir Nicholas said she was to stay here until he returned.

Fury has other things to worry about, my love.

Trieste.

I was sent to make sure you get safely to England.

You are the Old Man of the Knights Templar?

I am.

And you have something that you have brought with you?

On my cart.

It's a weapon, I understand?

In the wrong hands, all tools are weapons. In the right hands, everything is a weapon, or nothing is.

It's gold.

Very good. Gentlemen, we have our quarry.

I'm afraid the Queen of England is dead, old man. A much more reliable monarchy will be taking possession of your prize.

Kill the servant.

You two--bind his arms and legs and mouth. The rest of you, let's get the trunk off the cart.

I'm here to help you. Don't say anything. I'll get you safely to England...

Anything happening?

Nothing, Sir Nicholas. No signs of life.

Omnia Mutantur. All things change. Aye...

...but some changes are harder than I dreamed...

It is I, Nicholas Fury. *Open,* in the *King's* name!

Peter? Are you hurt, boy?

Only my pride. And my face is a little tender.

The guard last night was a trifle overzealous.

Carlos.

Hello, Nicholas. Would you like to talk about what troubles you?

This is not the time, Carlos. So, no.

The King has sent me here to take you and your pupils captive. Will you make it easy for me, or not?

Oh my sweet lord Jesus protect us.

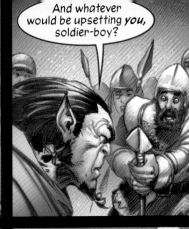

And whatever would be upsetting *you*, soldier-boy?

Have you never seen an Orkneyman before?

Ah, *yes*. I've been expecting you, young Petros.

And what message have you for me today?

The Inquisitor commends you on taking Javier and his monsters captive, and wishes to remind you of the second part of your obligation, Your Majesty--

--to turn the creatures over to the Inquisition.

My obligation? **MY OBLIGATION?**

I am the King of Scotland, soon to be crowned the rightful King of England. My obligation is to my conscience and to my God. Not to some Spanish offal-eater.

But what about *you*, pretty young man? Why don't you come and work for me?

I'll make you a Baron, or an Earl. Eh? You'll be a rich man, and an influential one.

Now *tell* me--*how* does the Inquisitor know that Javier has been captured? I have given the order, true...

Perhaps a little bird told him, Your Majesty.

And I hope that you will not take it amiss if, for now, at least, I keep my current position.

Well, Banner. The pretty young man left in quite a hurry.

Yes, Your Majesty.

"It glows, Reed. How does it glow? It casts light into the darkness. It is not gold. It is not glass. I have never seen anything like it."

I have told you my ideas of ways to make it give up its secrets... There must be a way to break it open, to get inside.

I could weaken it with Aqua Fortis... What do you suggest I try first?

Why don't you just lock it away in the darkness and *forget* about it, Otto? You don't know what it is or what it can do.

Everything you told me about it sounds *wrong*. Like it's not *from* here.

You are a coward and a fool, Reed. It is why YOU are the one who is locked away in the darkness. While I shall have light everlasting...

I cannot break it. The acids failed. Perhaps the galvanic energy will open it.

Power is all, Natasha. And when I control this power, I shall be unstoppable.

You are *already* unstoppable, Otto. All around us, the world falls into chaos. You write a new world on the ruins of the old.

But you must be careful.

There is no careful. There is no right, no wrong. There is only VON DOOM.

Hello, old friend. Are you well?

I am well, Donal. You?

I live.

"Good. The thing you were bringing to me?"

"It is here, in the castle. Doom has it, but he does not have it."

"For now, his attention has been distracted, by a curiosity--I brought it with me, hoping that it might distract attention."

What manner of curiosity?

A golden ball. It fell from the sky, some fifteen years ago and was a gift to the Order. I hope it will keep him occupied, while the Irishman and I get ourselves out of here. Somehow.

But it seems to me that Doom's prisoners do not escape.

Then we will have to remedy that.

"Hey! Old man! What's *wrong?*"

Are you all right? You were moaning in your dreams, and your heart was pounding fit to burst...

I am good. I saw Strange. He tells me that all will be well. They will free us. They will come.

Well now. Isn't *that* good to hear?

You know, if it wasn't for your dreams, old feller, given our situation, I can imagine I might feel almost discouraged.

Mistress **Clea?** Can I ask what you were talking about? The people who were elements...?

Certainly, Virginia. Let me see...

Sir Richard Reed was one of the most brilliant men who ever walked.

"Ten years back, he mounted an expedition to the New World, seeking not gold, or treasure, but knowledge.

"His ship, *the Fantastick,* was of his own design, captained by an old friend.

"There were others on the ship with him. A young adventurer, Master Storm, who had killed a man in a duel, they say, and had been sent abroad by the Queen...

"...and Storm's sister also, fleeing a man in London Town to whom she was betrothed, and whom she did not love.

There is a song the people sing. Let me see...

There were four brave souls rode the oceans abroad, T'was on the Fantastick they'd sail...

I've *heard* that song! The sailors on the *Virginia Maid* used to sing it! I could never understand the *story.*

Something about a light which changed them, and saving people from a huge monster or something.

"There is a sea called Sargasso, and it was on that sea that their ship was becalmed. It was adrift for days.

"Until, ahead of them they saw a curtain of light, which rent the world.

"The terrified crew thought their doom had come, and taking the ship's boat, rowed themselves away, but Reed and his two friends stayed with the ship, and so did the brave Captain.

"The *Fantastick* drifted through the curtain of light...

"...and when they reached land, they found themselves *changed*. Changed in ways no man could have imagined."

"Reed being Reed, they continued their journey westward, around the world. They would send messages home, from time to time. They were heroes who gave help to the weak and troubled."

"And then one day they *vanished*. The word went out that they were dead... but no man could say where they had died. And in time, hope faded as well.

"But hope, like heroes, can prove hard to kill."

When I touched it to your galvanic jar, it seemed as if faces swam in the golden surface.

Perhaps if there were a greater galvanic force... What if I were to put up a rod made of silver, above the castle, and then run it to the sphere...?

When lightning strikes, then we would see fireworks. Eh, Reed? Eh?

"You do not wish to play cards with the others?"

"I do not have the patience for it. To put it simply, Master Grey, I am scared, and angry. I fear for my life."

My wings are bound, and the cloth constricts me.

I am *tired* of looking like something I am not. I am *sick* of this pretense. And you, lad? How are *you*?

Very much the same.

Sir? Why do you talk to Master Grey, sir?

Scotius. *Please.*

I talk to Master Grey because I wish to, *sir*. I may talk to whom I please.

Indeed?

Indeed.

Do you wish to *fight* me, sir?

"If you could prove it..."

"...then *nothing* would stop me from going to Latveria myself, and ripping down Doom's mountain fastness *stone by stone* to free them all!"

"I can prove nothing. I am merely a mountebank. You said so yourself, to me, this morning, when I was a hundred miles away."

"Did you enjoy your bread and cheese?"

"He speaks the truth, Nicholas."

"How can you know for sure?"

"I don't. But I know that he believes he speaks truly. And I trust him."

"I see."

"Then I'll believe you, Strange. Although I fear that I am signing my death warrant."

"But to raise the army of men I would need to attack Latveria... to lead it across Europe, with all hands against us, would be impossible."

"And James would never give me an army. Nor could I get an army there fast enough."

"You are wrong, Nicholas."

You do **not** need an army. And it does not have to take weeks.

But when this is over, I want your word that you will find a safe place for my people. Somewhere neither James nor the Church will be able to harm us... those of us who are still alive.

And if we help you, then every hand will be against us all. My people, and yours.

You understand that, Nicholas? We will be traitors and fugitives and monsters forever.

I do not believe that the world is ending, Carlos. I neither like nor trust Doctor Stephen Strange. I failed to protect my Queen, and now I find myself betraying my new King.

But Reed was my friend. And **you** are my friend. You have my word.

Then I'll need a ship, the strongest, fastest that you have.

Fury--one last thing. The girl, Virginia. She is important. I believe that, in some way, she is causing this strange weather.

Hm. Then we should kill her.

I do not believe that would be a good idea.

No? It seems perfectly straight-forward to me.

I am certain it does.

At heart, Sir Nicholas, you are a military man, and so most problems can be dealt with by the death of those who trouble you.

But if the death of the girl also meant the death of the world, what then...?

Uhh...

Strange?

I...I am sorry. I don't know... what...I feel very...

You are white as chalk, Doctor.

Peter, make sure that Doctor Strange gets safely back to his home.

And then... go back to your village, to your Aunt and your Uncle. Get an honest job, lad, making chairs or building bridges. And try to forget that you ever worked for me.

Do you understand me?

No, sir.

You worked well and hard, lad. Fare you well.

And if you think that James is onto you, slit your throat. It'll be cleaner. God be with you.

I'm sorry... Peter...I cannot breathe...

Clea...

Sir? What should I...?

I--I'll get help!

"STEPHEN STRANGE. YOU ARE WELCOME HERE."

AND PERHAPS I DO OWE YOU SOMETHING OF AN EXPLANA-TION.

STEPHEN STRANGE, I AM AFRAID I CANNOT HELP YOU TO YOUR FEET. BUT IF YOU IMAGINE YOURSELF STANDING, THEN YOU WILL BE STANDING.

GOOD.

YOU HAVE NO LIPS TO SPEAK WITH, AND I AM USING MY MIND TO TALK DIRECTLY TO YOURS. DO YOU UNDER-STAND ME?

Where *am* I? Who are *you*? Are you an *angel*? A demon?

LET ME SEE...

YES. I MAY ANSWER ALL OF THOSE QUESTIONS. I AM NEITHER AN ANGEL NOR A DEMON. I AM A WATCHER. WE ARE ON YOUR PLANET'S MOON.

What's happening?

HMM... REPHRASE YOUR QUESTION TO MAKE IT MORE SPECIFIC AND THUS ANSWERABLE.

Well, you said you owed me an explanation. What am I doing on the *moon*? What manner of creature *are* you?

NO. THOSE WERE THE *WRONG* QUESTIONS. BUT I SHALL ANSWER THEM. YOU ARE ON THE MOON BECAUSE I NEEDED TO TALK WITH YOU. I AM A WATCHER, ONE OF MANY WATCHERS. WE OBSERVE EVENTS ACROSS THE UNIVERSE AND WE DO *NOT* INTERFERE.

AND I OWE YOU AN EXPLANATION.

IN THE LAST MONTH, I HAVE *PUSHED* YOUR MIND. I HAVE SPOKEN THROUGH YOUR MOUTH, AS IF I WERE YOU.

No. I'm sorry... I don't understand. Your concepts mean nothing. They're just words.

AH. MORE SIMPLE. I SHALL MAKE THE ATTEMPT.

ALL OTHER METHODS OF TIME-TRAVELLING THE WATCHERS HAVE OBSERVED UNTIL NOW MAKE USE OF THE VARIOUS PLIABLE PROPERTIES OF TIME. THEY TREAT TIME AS A RIVER.

AN EVENT ROUGHLY FOUR HUNDRED YEARS FROM NOW, ON THE OTHER HAND, WILL SIMPLY PUNCH A HOLE THROUGH TIME, A LITTLE MORE THAN A DOZEN YEARS AGO, AND DEPOSIT *SOMETHING* IN OUR RECENT PAST.

IT IS THE ARRIVAL OF THIS *SOMETHING* WHICH BEGINS THE CURRENT CYCLE OF DESTRUCTION.

What manner of something?

ALMOST CERTAINLY A HUMAN BEING. MY COLLEAGUES AND I HAVE OBSERVED AND PONDERED, AND WE ARE ALMOST ALL IN AGREEMENT ON THIS.

AND WE BELIEVE THAT THE DAMAGE TO THE FABRIC OF TIME BEGAN WITH THE ARRIVAL OF THIS ENTITY. WHATEVER IT IS.

You don't know?

I...WAS NOT WATCHING. I BLAME MYSELF, ALTHOUGH MY FELLOWS TELL ME THAT MY FAILURE WAS INEVITABLE. SOMETHING MAY HAVE STOPPED ME.

Who would stop you watching?

THE UNIVERSE FOLLOWS CERTAIN LAWS, STEPHEN STRANGE, AND, LIKE YOU, I AM A CREATURE OF THE UNIVERSE. SOME LAWS I UNDERSTAND, SOME I DO NOT. I AM YOUNG, AS WE RECKON THINGS.

IN TRUTH, YOURS IS A YOUNG SOLAR SYSTEM, AND IT IS THE ONLY ONE I HAVE WATCHED.

AND THERE IS SOMETHING ELSE I DO NOT UNDERSTAND.

EVERYTHING HAS ITS SEASON. IN SPRING, THE WORLD BRINGS FORTH BLOSSOMS. IN CHERRY SEASON, YOU GET CHERRIES.

BUT A SEASON HAS DAWNED OVER THREE HUNDRED YEARS EARLY: A SEASON OF HEROES AND MARVELS. MY OWN CONCLUSION--SEVERAL OF MY COLLEAGUES LAUGH AT ME--IS THAT THE TWO ARE CONNECTED.

THAT THE UNIVERSE FIGHTS TO SAVE ITSELF.

TO SAVE EVERYTHING, THE HEROES HAVE COME.

THE HYPOTHESIS MY STAIDER COLLEAGUES PREFER IS THAT THE ARRIVAL OF THE ENTITY THEY REFER TO AS THE FORERUNNER IS, IN ITSELF, THE SIGNAL TO THE UNIVERSE FOR THE SEASON OF MARVELS TO BEGIN.

AND THAT ENTITY'S ARRIVAL ALSO CREATED THE SIMULTANEITY.

You said you were not permitted to interfere. Yes?

THAT IS CORRECT.

But you brought me here, and told me this.

You are obviously interfering. Why?

A VALID QUESTION. I HAVE CONSULTED WITH MY FELLOWS. THE CONSENSUS OF OPINION WAS THAT IF THE TOTALITY OF ALL UNIVERSES CAME TO AN END, THERE WOULD BE NOTHING LEFT FOR US TO WATCH.

AND THAT WOULD BE...REGRETTABLE.

THUS, THE SMALLEST AMOUNT OF INTERFERENCE MAY BE PERMITTED.

THE SIMULTANEITY MUST BE CLOSED. THE FORERUNNER MUST BE RETURNED, OR DESTROYED.

And how do I do that? How do I find this "Forerunner"? Where is this "simultaneity" you keep talking about?

I WILL **SHOW** YOU, STEPHEN. YOU WILL SEE WHAT I KNOW THROUGH MY EYES. YOU WILL SEE **EVERYTHING**.

BUT I AM STILL A WATCHER, AND I AM STILL BOUND BY THE CODES AND OATHS OF MY KIND...

"THERE IS ONLY ONE INJUNCTION I MUST LAY UPON YOU, STEPHEN. IT IS THIS:

"WHILE YOU LIVE, YOU MAY SAY NOTHING OF WHAT YOU KNOW TO ANY SOUL. YOU MAY NOT ACT IN ANY WAY UPON WHAT YOU KNOW.

"LIKE ME, YOU ARE CONDEMNED ONLY TO WATCH."

...only to watch...

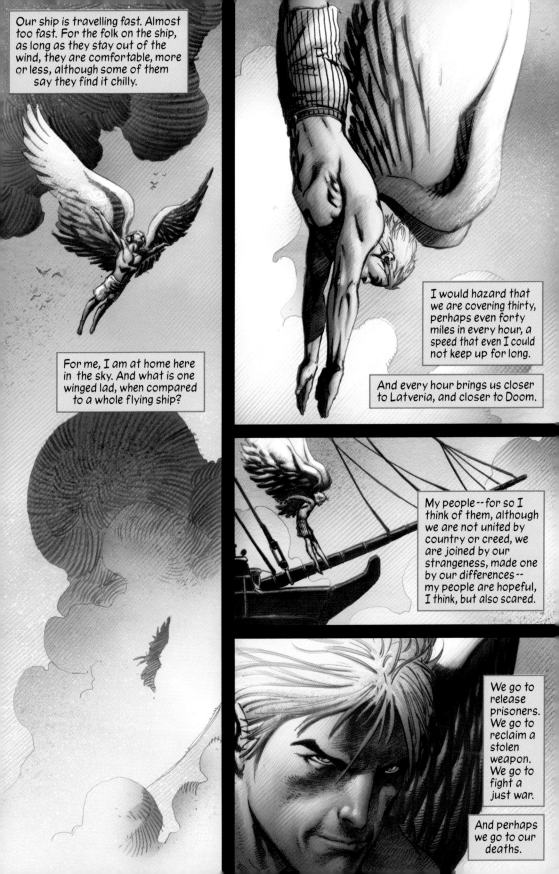

Our ship is travelling fast. Almost too fast. For the folk on the ship, as long as they stay out of the wind, they are comfortable, more or less, although some of them say they find it chilly.

For me, I am at home here in the sky. And what is one winged lad, when compared to a whole flying ship?

I would hazard that we are covering thirty, perhaps even forty miles in every hour, a speed that even I could not keep up for long.

And every hour brings us closer to Latveria, and closer to Doom.

My people--for so I think of them, although we are not united by country or creed, we are joined by our strangeness, made one by our differences-- my people are hopeful, I think, but also scared.

We go to release prisoners. We go to reclaim a stolen weapon. We go to fight a just war.

And perhaps we go to our deaths.

But if we die, it will be a death of our choosing. A good death, if such a thing can be.

We follow rivers and hills, small villages and farms. Sir Nicholas knows Europe like he knows his own face, and he is our navigator.

Dougan, his man, is loyal to Fury, although like all of us, he is scared.

We avoid cities and towns, where we can.

Master Grey says that, while he can keep the ship moving, he doubts that he could raise it again, so we travel without stopping, hour after hour, towards the south and towards the east.

Some of us have slept below decks, but John Grey has not slept, and neither has our leader, Carlos Javier, who sits beside the boy, and feeds his powers with his own.

Because I tell the *truth*.

There is a flying ship coming here. It is manned with witchbreed creatures and demons. They seek to make war on you.

There has never been any love lost between Latveria and the Inquisition. Did not your own Grand Inquisitor condemn my father's breeding studies as heretical?

If he *did*, then think of this as his olive branch.

If this business of flying witch-breed is true, why have I not heard of it?

Their ship moves too *fast*. It is outpacing your fastest messengers.

I have some very fast messengers.

It seems you are telling the truth, my friend.

Now, I think it would be best for all of us if you were to remain here, in safety, until these pirates are dealt with. Eh?

GUARDS!

The first order of business is to get you all down there, and to destroy their weapons, before they blow us from the sky.

Angel, you carry Scotius. Once you've got him down, come back for Sir Nicholas.

But he's only a--

Only a human? Perhaps. But I'm dangerous enough, in my own way.

You're thinking that I hate you, Master Somerisle.

And you have given me no cause to love you.

But I have no plans to drop you. Rest easy on that score.

Watch out!

What?

I thank you.

Just get me down safely.

Robbie--can you create an ice-bridge from here to the castle top?

I do not believe so. It's too far--I need the air to be wetter. If only there was rain, or mist, I could do so much...

You can still deflect cannonballs. Do so. I shall be in the minds of the cannoneers, showing them our ship is lower, or higher, than they believe. But some may still slip through...

...so for now you and Henry shall stay here, to defend the ship.

Against what? You have not taught me to catch cannon-balls.

Against them.

Ah...*this!*

This is living!

What are they?

Doom's creatures.

From those who have much...

...to give...

...much is demanded...

From those who have much...

...to give...

...much is demanded...

I wouldn't know what manner of monster it is that Doom keeps in his basement, but we owe it our *thanks*...

...for loosening the bolts that held our chains, and for what it's done to this wall.

There.

Matthew?

Yes, Donal?

How will we get down to the court-yard?

We wrap your chains around me...

...and you hold *very* tight...

Well, the way I see it, we have *two* options. We could call a guard, talk him into opening the cell door, overpower him, go down through the castle--*hiding, fighting,* all that... but it's an awful lot of work.

So let's do it the *easy* way.

Which is?

Brother John. Oh my poor *brother...*

...he is a *monster* to keep you so, and *use* you so...

Even with his ears covered, the crash of thunder is deafening: louder than the cannons, louder than the monster in the dungeon...

...it leaves him disoriented, although he can still smell the ozone lightning flash.

That was close, he thinks, as the rain begins to pour from a previously cloudless sky...

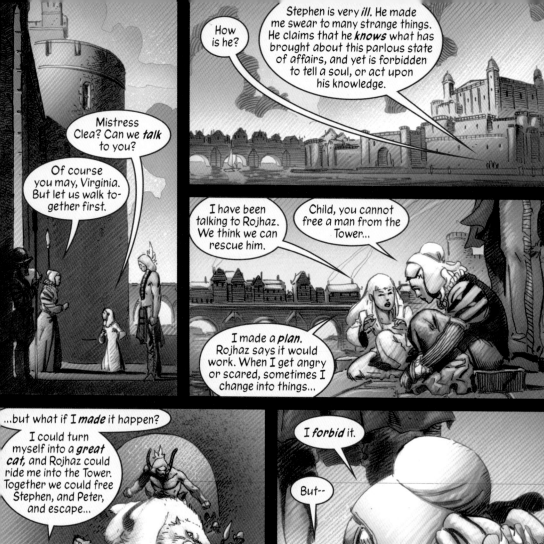

Mistress Clea? Can we *talk* to you?

Of course you may, Virginia. But let us walk together first.

How is he?

Stephen is very *ill*. He made me swear to many strange things. He claims that he *knows* what has brought about this parlous state of affairs, and yet is forbidden to tell a soul, or act upon his knowledge.

I have been talking to Rojhaz. We think we can rescue him.

Child, you cannot free a man from the Tower...

I made a *plan*. Rojhaz says it would work. When I get angry or scared, sometimes I change into things...

...but what if I *made* it happen? I could turn myself into a *great cat*, and Rojhaz could ride me into the Tower. Together we could free Stephen, and Peter, and escape...

I *forbid* it.

But--

If Stephen were rescued by supernatural means, then James would murder *every* suspected witch, magician, cunning-man and wise-woman in Britain.

The King's fears must be allowed to die away, not be fanned into hatred and war.

We can't just let it happen... *Perhaps* King James will be *merciful*.

He won't.

You made me swear. And I *swore*, Stephen, as I swore I would be yours when you freed me, far beyond the veils of this world.

But it hurt me more than anything has ever hurt me.

And I would follow you into the darkness, now. I do not *wish* to *stay.*

Clea. There is but little time before the darkness takes me... There was a ...**compulsion** placed upon my lips--that I could not speak of what I learned, while I *lived.*

The Forerunner came here from the future. Its arrival made other things happen: things that should not have happened for hundreds of years happened because the Forerunner was here.

As a stone, dropped into a pond, creates ripples that spread, so the Forerunner's presence cast its influence into the past and the future.

The Forerunner is the first. We all follow it...even you. Even me.

You must send the Forerunner back.

When I was a Queen, far from here...

...my people said the dead would speak only in riddles, Stephen.

I am speaking as clearly as I can. It came here from another time. The machine that brought it has already been destroyed.

It must be returned, by the same gate it came through...

You must take it back to America.

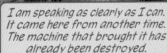

She had begged not to be cast into the ocean.

I was asked if I could be part of her funeral pyre, and I said *I could not*. I felt as if I had lost not one friend, but two.

The girl that everyone else saw, the boy that I had wanted so to believe in.

I imagined them all *laughing* at me. I wondered if they understood my shame.

In my place, John Storm took her corpse, and, burning, flew with her so high that we could barely see them.

Then he let her *fall*...

And while Master Javier muttered his God-be-with-yous, Somerisle took the rubies from his eyes, and he stared at the heavens.

There were tears on his cheeks, and I wondered how those eyes, which burn like suns, could cry.

She smoked and glowed. Then she erupted into light, burned so brightly I wanted to look away, but I did not look away. I *could* not.

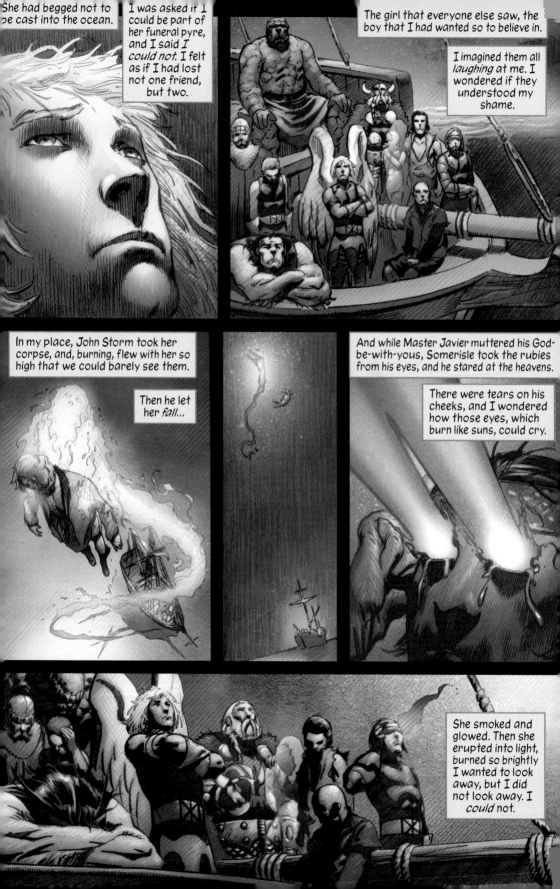

I imagined something. That in the light of the dead girl burning, *something* spread its wings...

Something huge. Somethind strange. Something *beautiful*.

And then...

And then there was nothing left.

Nothing but ashes.

1602.

On board the *Virginia Maid*, sailing to Roanoke.

Rojhaz speaks:

My name...

I was born... will be born... maybe I *won't* be born... in the year 1920. Over three hundred years from now. My name was Steven Rogers.

Is. Steve. Rogers.

I'm sorry. So much of this is like a dream...

"There's a war coming, we called it World War Two, it started when I was about twenty, and I was given a... a serum. A *physic*, yes?"

"Stuff to make me big, and strong, and fast."

"And it *did*.

"I was a fighting machine, and a good one, and more than that."

I saved lives.

I... I couldn't save *everyone*.

Then, end of the war, I lost a couple of decades. After they thawed me out. I was... I was a hero. I remember some of it. A lot of it's kind of mixed up...

"I fought for *America*. My country.

"I protected America. Life, liberty and the pursuit of happiness.

"*Democracy.* Not something you people have seen much of yet. But it's worth fighting for..."

That's what I do.

Will do...

Did...

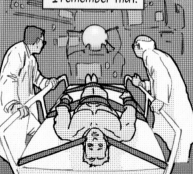

"After that, things got kind of foggy, for a long time.

"I wasn't certain where I was, or who I was. I couldn't understand the words. Or the people. I told them my name...

"They thought I was from another tribe... I guess, in a way, they were right.

"They let me stay. They fed me...

"Nothing mattered. And then the white people came across the great water, and I found them starving, and I fed them.

"And then there was *Virginia*..."

She was a baby then. But I knew what she was. What she represented. What she *meant*. My America...

I knew I had to protect her. To guard her. To fight for her, if I had to.

I wasn't going to let *her* die.

I failed before.

I wasn't going to fail again.

It's a good little village, Carlos. You'll like it. Master Ananias has given us a cottage, and the village hall, for lodgings.

Now, what did you want to tell me?

Only *this*.

Three ships are coming, Niccolo. I *feel* them. Each brings unfinished business.

"The *first* ship contains someone dead, yet not dead. A *friend*."

"It also carries a witch, a changeling, and...someone else. Someone whose mind is closed to me."

"Another ship contains James's agents. They are coming to *kill* you, Niccolo."

"Good. That's what I would have done if I were James. Sensible."

One of them is the boy, Peter.

That sly old fox. Well, let us see where this takes us.

And the *third* ship?

"More unfinished business. *Mine.* An enemy who was once, long ago, a friend."

The *Inquisitor?*

Yes.

Hm. Well, perhaps we could arrange with Reed to *destroy* his ship before he ever reaches land. *Burn* it, perhaps...?

No, Niccolo.

If we murder them, we would be no better than they are. Let me think on this: a solution will present itself.

You all know my husband.

I can assure you that this is not pleasant for either of us. Now...you must ask questions.

Hello Strange. Good to see you, in...well, obviously rather trying circumstances.

Hello Reed.

I have died, that others may have their chance at life.

Do not ignore my words.

Get on with it.

Is that a question, Nicholas?

A question. Very well.

Tell us, Doctor. What say you: is the *world* truly *ending?*

Something-- a person--from the future came here, fifteen years ago.

This event damaged the nature of time itself; and, because time and space are one, it will soon destroy everything...

Strange... if I may interrupt you there?

Obviously something is *out* with time. Just as obviously there is an increasing fragility to *existence.*

To a Natural Philosopher, it is obvious that the phenomenon that drew us all here can be reduced to four fundamental problems.

This is my *country*. They need me.

I *can't* leave them.

We don't have to make the same mistakes again. We're here at the birth of a nation...of a dream.

Nobody has to *die*.

We can work together to *protect* them. My *people*.

One girl, currently in the form of a hound, and a handful of settlers? Your people?

They're *America*. One day they'll be America. And I...I'll make them proud to be Americans.

If you don't return to your own time, there won't be *anything*!

Don't you understand?

I... I *know* you, Fury. I know *all* those people who have come to Roanoke.

I knew you all, a long time ago. I remember *Reed*, and *Sue* and *Javier*, and *all* of them. I...remember...

...you people...I've known you for *a long* time...

Rojhaz... come down, and we can talk about this.

I won't hurt you.

No closer.

Look. You say you knew me-- someone like me. In another time. In another world. Tell me--would that *other* Nicholas Fury *betray* you? Would he *lie* to you?

Think about it.

I...

I'll come down.

It's *Fury*.

But--what is he doing?

What does it *matter?* He's here. So are we.

It's our time.

THERE IS A NOISE THEN, SO LOUD
IT FILLS THE WORLD. THE SOUND
OF A UNIVERSE SCREAMING IN PAIN.
THE SOUND OF A WORLD DYING.

AND AFTER
THAT, SILENCE.

SO. IT IS
OVER.

I FEEL TIME
RECONFIGURE
ITSELF.

THE COLONY AT ROANOKE SIMPLY STARVES,
THEIR FIRST WINTER IN THE HARSH NEW
CONTINENT. A HANDFUL OF SURVIVORS ARE
RESCUED BY THE NATIVES.

VIRGINIA DARE WILL DIE IN THE FORM OF
A WHITE DEER, HER OWN NAME ON HER
LIPS AS SHE TRANSFORMS FOR THE FINAL
TIME, NEVER NOW TO BECOME QUEEN OF
ANYTHING...

TIME HEALS,
AND IS HEALED.

ALL WILL COME INTO EXISTENCE
IN ITS PROPER TIME. ONE SMALL
POSSIBILITY HAS ENDED, THAT
EVERYTHING ELSE MAY EXIST.

EVERYTHING I DID, I DID FOR
GOOD REASON. AND YET...

AND YET...

IF THIS IS RIGHT, WHY
DO I FEEL SO...EMPTY?

AND, WITH MOUNTING FASCINATION...

...ONCE MORE...

...I BEGIN TO WATCH.

"So, we are still here.

"Nothing has changed..."

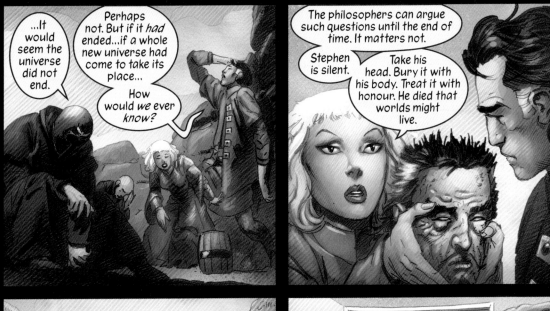

...It would seem the universe did not end.

Perhaps not. But if it *had* ended...if a whole new universe had come to take its place...

How would *we* ever know?

The philosophers can argue such questions until the end of time. It matters not.

Stephen is silent.

Take his head. Bury it with his body. Treat it with honour. He died that worlds might live.

It is, finally, time for me to go home.

Good-bye.

'My *own* suggestion, Javier, would be to declare the colony independent of England. Your people can guard the coast.

"James is a long way away; he lacks the coffers or the will to prosecute a war so far from home."

And will you be their King, Reed?

I do not believe that there will be any more call for Kings or for Queens.

I shall propose to Master Dare that we make the colony a place where people--people of *all* shapes and talents-- can prosper...

Peter?

Virginia? It *is* you! Did you see where Master Banner went? He was trying to protect me from the strange light...

I think I fell asleep.

I don't *remember.* I saw only the light. And then Fury and Rojhaz were gone...

Banner will tell James that I stopped him killing Fury. I *know* he will. I am a dead man if I go home.

My Uncle, my Aunt...

We can get them out of England. Somehow. I know we can. And you can stay with us. Until then.

Stay with me and my father.

I think... I think I would *like* that...

OW!

That spider. It bit the back of my hand.

Well, it's not the end of the world. I'll put a poultice on it.

Come on, Peter. Let's go home.

FINIS